858958

LEBRON JAMES

BY BRIAN HOWELL

Published by ABDO Publishing Company, 8000 West 78th Street, Edina, Minnesota 55439. Copyright © 2011 by Abdo Consulting Group, Inc. International copyrights reserved in all countries. No part of this book may be reproduced in any form without written permission from the publisher. SportsZone™ is a trademark and logo of ABDO Publishing Company.

Printed in the United States of America,
North Mankato, Minnesota
112010
012011

 THIS BOOK CONTAINS AT LEAST 10% RECYCLED MATERIALS.

Editor: Matt Tustison
Copy Editor: Susan M. Freese
Interior Design and Production: Craig Hinton
Cover Design: Craig Hinton

Photo Credits: Charlie Riedel/AP Images, cover, title; Tony Dejak/file/AP Images, 4; J Pat Carter/AP Images, 7; Tony Dejak/AP Images, 8; Amy Sancetta /AP Images, 11; Mark Duncan/ AP Images, 12; Terry Gilliam/AP Images, 14; Mark Duncan /AP Images, 17; Paul Vernon /AP Images, 18; Tony Dejak/AP Images, 20; Steve Yeater /AP Images, 23; Duane Burleson /AP Images, 24; Phil Long/AP Images, 26; Scott Shaw/The Cleveland Plain Dealer/AP Images, 29

Library of Congress Cataloging-in-Publication Data
Howell, Brian, 1974-
  LeBron James : basketball icon / by Brian Howell.
     p. cm. — (Playmakers)
  ISBN 978-1-61714-746-3
  1. James, LeBron—Juvenile literature. 2. Basketball players—United States—Biography—Juvenile literature. I. Title.
  GV884.J36H69 2011
  796.323092—dc22
  [B]
                              2010046355

TABLE OF CONTENTS

LeBron James

CHAPTER 1

THE MVP

The National Basketball Association (NBA) is full of great players. Kobe Bryant of the Los Angeles Lakers, Kevin Durant of the Oklahoma City Thunder, Dwyane Wade of the Miami Heat, and Dwight Howard of the Orlando Magic are some of the best. But LeBron James might be the very best. He stands out even when playing with these stars.

The NBA's All-Star Game brings together all the best players in the league for one game. In the

LeBron James dunks in 2010. That year, the Cavs' star was the NBA's MVP for a second season in a row.

2010 All-Star Game, James was amazing. He scored 25 points. He helped his team, the Eastern Conference All-Stars, beat the Western Conference All-Stars 141–139.

James has been one of the NBA's top players since joining the league in 2003. He played for the Cleveland Cavaliers for his first seven seasons. He was named the NBA's Most Valuable Player (MVP) for the 2008–09 season. He won the MVP Award again for 2009–10.

James was 24 years old when he won his first MVP Award. Only two other MVPs in NBA history were younger than him. Wes Unseld was 23 when he won the award in 1969 playing for the Baltimore Bullets. Moses Malone was 24 but 90 days younger than James when he won his first MVP Award in 1979 with the Houston Rockets.

There aren't many athletes in the world who can match James's ability. He is 6 feet, 8 inches tall, and he weighs 250 pounds. He's big, but he can jump high and run fast.

Soon after winning his second MVP Award, James had a big decision to make. He went into the summer of 2010 as

James, *left*, and new teammate Dwyane Wade attend a Heat event in July 2010. James had just signed to play with Miami.

a free agent. A free agent is a player who can join any team. James had played for the Cavaliers all his years in the NBA. He was a hometown hero in Cleveland. That city is only 40 miles (64 km) from Akron, Ohio, which is where he grew up. But several other teams wanted James to play for them.

Although James still loved his hometown, he decided to leave the Cavaliers. He signed to play with the Heat. Joining Miami would allow James to play with his friend Wade.

LeBron James

CHAPTER 2

GROWING UP

LeBron Raymone James was born on December 30, 1984, in Akron, Ohio. He faced challenges from the very beginning of his life. LeBron's mother, Gloria, was 16 years old and still in high school when he was born. LeBron's father wasn't around when he was a child.

LeBron's grandmother helped to raise him when he was very young. But she died just a few days before his third birthday. That left LeBron and Gloria

James hugs his mother, Gloria, after the Cavaliers beat the Magic in a 2009 playoff game.

LeBron got his first basketball when he was almost three years old. He received a mini ball and hoop as a Christmas present. He had fun playing and especially loved to dunk the ball.

on their own. LeBron and his mother moved around a lot. That made it difficult for him to make friends at school.

Despite these tough times, LeBron has always been close to his mother. He knows that she did her best to take care of him. "My mom kept food in my mouth and clothes on my back," he has said. "My mother is my everything. Always has been. Always will be."

Gloria always made sure LeBron was well cared for. Sometimes that meant having him live with other people. During fourth grade, LeBron began living with his football coach, Frankie Walker, and the coach's family. LeBron still saw his mother a lot, but the Walkers helped him grow up. Living with the Walkers helped LeBron focus on school.

James poses with his mother, Gloria, after he received the NBA MVP Award in May 2009.

James watches the teams warm up before a Cleveland Browns game in 2008. As a youngster, James played football.

During this time, LeBron also became involved with sports. He didn't start off playing basketball, though. His first sport was football. And right away, he became a star player. He caught a lot of passes. He scored 19 touchdowns the first year he played. He kept playing football until eleventh grade.

Soon after LeBron started playing football, he discovered basketball. It didn't take long to see that he was something special on the court. Adults noticed that LeBron was a quick learner. That helped him develop as a player. He also spent hours practicing. From the time LeBron first played basketball, he worked hard to be the best.

LeBron and his childhood friend Dru Joyce III played basketball a lot. They often played against each other at the Joyces' house. And they both hated to lose. Dru's father said, "They were so competitive, I had them stop after the sixth grade. They were best friends, but they kept wanting to fight each other after those games."

In fifth grade, LeBron joined a team called the Northeast Ohio Shooting Stars. The Stars played in the Amateur Athletic Union (AAU). Dru Joyce II was the coach of the Stars. Joyce's son, Dru Joyce III, was also on the team. LeBron and the younger Dru became good friends. Two of their teammates were Sian Cotton and Willie McGee.

LeBron, Dru, Sian, and Willie were all excellent players. They called themselves the "Fab Four." Together, they won more than 200 games.

CHAPTER 3

BECOMING A STAR

When it was time to start high school, LeBron James and his friends wanted to be together. LeBron, Dru Joyce III, Sian Cotton, and Willie McGee all decided to attend St. Vincent-St. Mary High School in Akron. The Fab Four wanted to make sure they could play on the same team. They would play for the Irish.

LeBron scored 15 points in his first basketball game in high school. After that, he just got better.

LeBron shoots for St. Vincent-St. Mary High School of Akron, Ohio, in 2002.

LeBron was both a football and a basketball star in high school. In football, he played wide receiver. He was named to the Ohio All-State team as a sophomore.

He helped his team win all 27 of its games that season. LeBron scored 25 points for the Irish in the state championship game.

When LeBron was a sophomore, he helped lead the Irish to another state championship. The team finished the season with a 26–1 record. LeBron received the Ohio Mr. Basketball Award after this outstanding season. LeBron and the Irish went 23–4 the next season. But they lost in the state championship game. When LeBron was a senior, the Irish went 25–1 and won another state crown.

LeBron played so well in high school that he became known around the United States. He was called "King James." St. Vincent-St. Mary played some of the best teams in the country. One of them was Oak Hill Academy of Virginia.

LeBron is fired up during St. Vincent-St. Mary's game against Oak Hill Academy in December 2002.

James and former St. Vincent-St. Mary teammates Brandon Weems, *left*, and Willie McGee, *right*, visit in 2009.

More than 11,000 fans attended the game between St. Vincent-St. Mary and Oak Hill. It was also broadcast on ESPN television. LeBron put on quite a show. He scored 31 points and had 13 rebounds. The Irish won by 20 points.

LeBron and the Irish played a lot of strong teams during his senior year of high school. At the end of the year, the newspaper *USA Today* named the Irish the national champions.

LeBron was on the cover of *Sports Illustrated* magazine when he was a junior in high school at St. Vincent-St. Mary. The magazine had the headline "The Chosen One." By this time, NBA scouts were already watching LeBron.

This meant they were considered the best high school team in the United States.

LeBron was a star in high school. He and the Irish traveled around the United States to play. The team's games were on television. Fans packed the gyms to see LeBron play. He didn't disappoint anyone. Those who came saw a great basketball player.

NBA Hall of Fame player Bill Walton was at the Oak Hill game. He watched LeBron take control of the court. "This guy has the complete package," Walton said after the game. "What I saw tonight was a special basketball player. It was an eye-opening experience for me."

By the time LeBron was a junior, his talent was sky high. When he was a senior, it was clear that he would skip college and turn professional. The NBA wanted LeBron. He would soon take the court with the best players in the world.

LeBron James

CHAPTER 4

GUIDING THE CAVS

LeBron James finished his career at St. Vincent-St. Mary High School in the spring of 2003. At the same time, the Cleveland Cavaliers finished the season with the worst record in the NBA.

The NBA held its draft in June 2003. The draft is an event in which the teams in the league take turns picking new players.

In the 2003 NBA Draft, most teams thought James was the best player available. The Cavaliers

James holds up his new jersey on June 27, 2003. The day before, the Cavaliers drafted him.

had the first pick in the draft. They selected James. He was about to become a hometown hero in Cleveland.

James was only 18 years old when he joined the Cavs. It was clear from the beginning that he belonged in the NBA. In his first regular-season game, he scored 25 points and had nine assists and six rebounds. This was just the start of a remarkable rookie season. James scored an average of 20.9 points per game and was the league's Rookie of the Year. James did even better the next year. He scored 27.2 points per game. He was chosen to play in the NBA All-Star Game for the first time.

James had only one disappointment during his first two seasons with the Cavs: The team didn't make it to the playoffs. But that would change. During the next five seasons, James would lead the Cavs to the playoffs every year.

During the 2007 playoffs, LeBron helped the Cavaliers get all the way to the NBA Finals. But before playing in that championship round, the team had to win the Eastern Conference title. That meant beating the Detroit Pistons. The Cavs lost the first two games to the Pistons. But they won the next four games to take the playoff series.

James passes during his first NBA regular-season game on October 29, 2003, in Sacramento, California.

James played remarkably well in Game 5 against the Pistons. He had 48 points, nine rebounds, and seven assists. He scored 29 of Cleveland's final 30 points to help the Cavaliers win in double overtime.

The Cavaliers went on to play in the 2007 NBA Finals, but they lost to the San Antonio Spurs. San Antonio won all four games.

The Pistons' Tayshaun Prince, *right*, defends James in a 2007 playoff game. James led the Cavs to victory with 48 points.

James seemed to improve every year. He got better at passing and rebounding. He also improved at playing defense.

James also became a solid leader. He made sure the Cavaliers became a winning team. In the 2008–09 season, the Cavs had the best record in the NBA at 66–16. The Cavs also had the best record the next season, finishing 61–21. But his team didn't advance to the NBA Finals either season. The Cavaliers lost to the Orlando Magic in the 2009 playoffs and to the Boston Celtics the next year.

Through 2010, James had played in the Olympics twice for the United States. In 2004, he helped Team USA win the bronze medal in Athens, Greece. Then in 2008, he helped the team win the gold in Beijing, China. James scored 14 points in the championship game as the United States beat Spain 118–107.

By the end of the 2009–10 season, James had played with the Cavaliers for seven years. He had helped them become one of the best teams in the league. He still had an important goal to achieve: to win an NBA championship.

James thought that playing for another team might help him do that. He could change teams because he had become a free agent. So he made the difficult decision to move on.

On July 8, 2010, James joined the Miami Heat. This gave him the opportunity to play with two of his friends, Dwyane Wade and Chris Bosh. James was excited about having this chance. He said, "We feel like we can be great together."

Cavaliers fans were upset. But Heat fans were thrilled to have James on their team. Many people who followed the NBA predicted the Heat would win the next league championship with James on the team.

LeBron James

GIVING BACK

LeBron James's childhood was difficult at times. He was thankful to have the Walker family's help. When James became a star NBA player, he decided he would help others too.

James started the LeBron James Family Foundation. The foundation helps families in need, especially single-parent families. In 2005, the foundation gave 1,000 backpacks to kids in Akron and Cleveland. The backpacks were full of school supplies.

James gets ready before the start of the King for Kids charity bike-a-thon in August 2010 in Akron, Ohio.

Gloria James, LeBron's mom, helped create the foundation with LeBron. She said, "Starting the school year with a pencil, paper, and something to put it in was one thing I made sure LeBron had every school year. Now we want to help others by providing those same things."

James believes it's important to help others. That's why he started the LeBron James Family Foundation. "What I do with basketball only lasts during the season, but the work we do with the foundation goes on non-stop," he has said. "We want to keep building hopes and dreams in the lives of children and families."

James also puts on the King for Kids charity bike-a-thon in Akron every year. The event supports physical fitness for kids.

One of James's most special moments came around Thanksgiving in 2007. He invited 800 people from Cleveland to Quicken Loans Arena, where the Cavaliers play. Many of the people were homeless. James provided all of them with a Thanksgiving dinner. Then he treated them to a movie. He also gave the people gift cards to buy groceries. "I know I

Families react to James's appearance at a Thanksgiving dinner event that he hosted in 2007 in Cleveland.

can't fulfill every kid's dream," James said. "But I'm thankful I can do something like this, especially during the holidays."

James has spent countless hours helping other people since becoming a professional basketball player. He knows he is lucky, and he enjoys giving to those who aren't as lucky. Both on and off the court, he has proven himself a hero.

FUN FACTS AND QUOTES

- LeBron James's favorite player when he was growing up was Chicago Bulls star Michael Jordan. Jordan wore number 23. James wore the same number during high school and during his seven seasons with the Cleveland Cavaliers.

- James is a father. He and his girlfriend, Savannah Brinson, have two sons together: LeBron James Jr. and Bryce Maximus James.

- James does a lot of commercials and other advertisements to endorse products. But his biggest endorsement is for Nike. James even has his own line of Nike shoes.

- James said he loves spending time with kids. "I make sure I take care of the kids first," he has said. "If I see a kid, I'm going to try to spend as much time with him as I can."

WEB LINKS

To learn more about LeBron James, visit ABDO Publishing Company online at **www.abdopublishing.com**. Web sites about James are featured on our Book Links page. These links are routinely monitored and updated to provide the most current information available.

GLOSSARY

challenge
Something that can be difficult to complete.

charity
A generous action done to help others.

discover
To find or learn about something new.

dunk
In basketball, a play in which the ball is slammed directly through the hoop.

improve
To get better at something.

league
In sports, a group of teams that play against each other. Professional basketball teams are part of the National Basketball Association (NBA).

practice
To repeat something to get better at it.

professional
In sports, someone who is hired and gets paid to play his or her sport.

rebound
In basketball, to get the ball after a missed shot.

remarkable
Something that's amazing or unusual.

rookie
In sports, a player who is in his or her first season.

INDEX

FURTHER RESOURCES

Christopher, Matt, and Stephanie Peters. *On the Court with . . . LeBron James*. New York: Little, Brown Books for Young Readers, 2008.

Jones, Ryan. *King James: Believe the Hype*. New York: St. Martin's Press, 2005.

Wallace Sharp, Anne. *People in the News: LeBron James*. Farmington Hills, MI: Lucent Books, 2008.